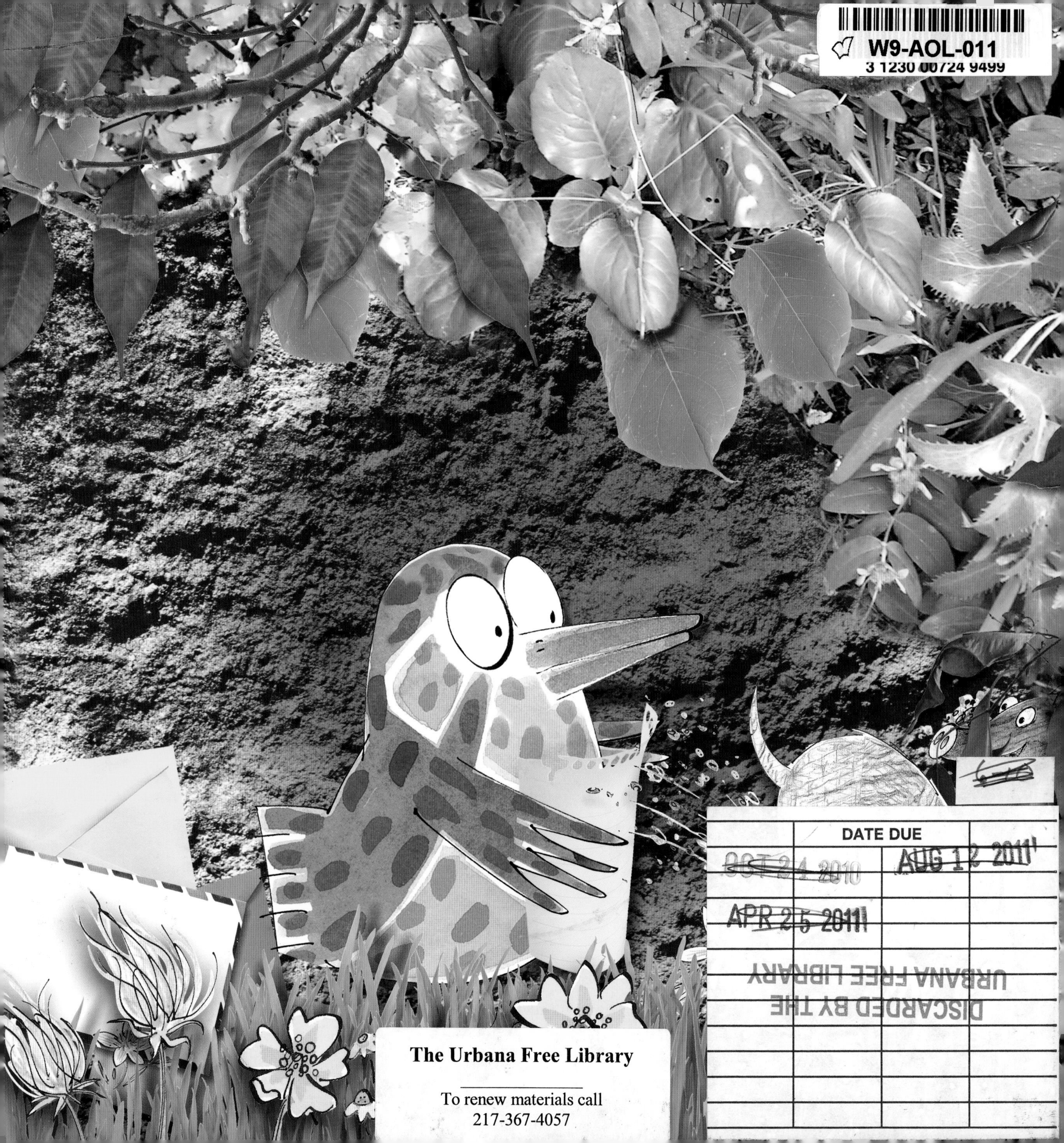

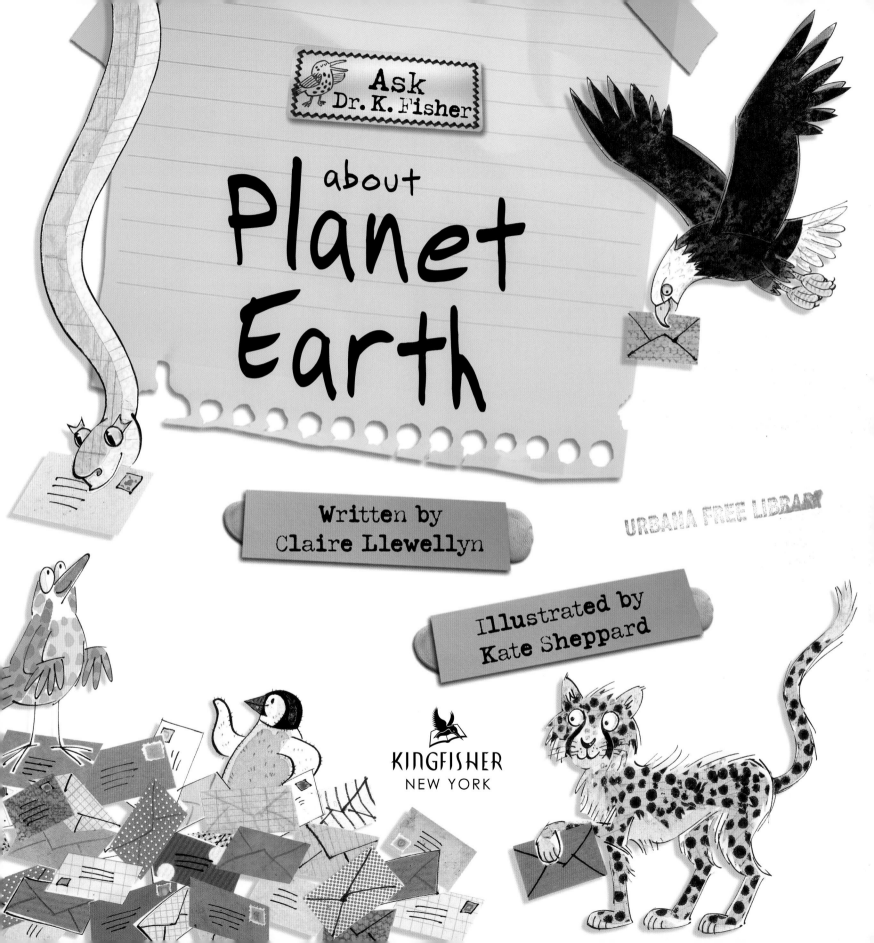

Ask Dr. K. Fisher

about Planet Earth

Written by
Claire Llewellyn

Illustrated by
Kate Sheppard

KINGFISHER
NEW YORK

Claire

Kate

KINGFISHER
LONDON & NEW YORK

Copyright © 2009 by Kingfisher
Text and concept © Claire Llewellyn 2009
Published in the United States by Kingfisher,
175 Fifth Ave., New York, NY 10010
Kingfisher is an imprint of Macmillan Children's Books, London.

Consultant: David Burnie

Distributed in the U.S. by Macmillan,
175 Fifth Ave., New York, NY 10010
Distributed in Canada by H.B. Fenn and Company Ltd.,
34 Nixon Road, Bolton, Ontario L7E 1W2

Library of Congress Cataloging-in-Publication data
has been applied for.

ISBN: 978-0-7534-6304-8

Kingfisher books are available for special promotions and
premiums. For details contact: Special Markets Department,
Macmillan, 175 Fifth Avenue, New York, NY 10010.

For more information, please visit www.kingfisherpublications.com

Printed in China
9 8 7 6 5 4 3 2 1
1TR/0509/LFG/SCHOY/157MA/C

For Annie and Kenneth,
fondest love—K. S.

Kingfisher

175 Fifth Avenue

New York, NY 10010

www.kingfisherpublications.com

Ask Dr. K. Fisher about . . .

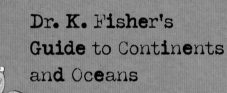
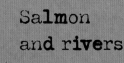

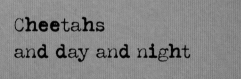

bush baby

Digging for success?

Dear Dr. K. Fisher,
I'm an aardvark and King of the burrowers. Just to give you some idea, my burrow right now is so deep that a tall tree could easily fit inside it. Some friends of mine have challenged me to burrow to the other side of the world. I figure I can do it all right but would be grateful for any tips.

Quietly Confident,
in the Kalahari Desert

THE DESERT
MAR 26
MAIL

Dr. K. Fisher

1 Diving-in-the-Water

Birdsville 54321

aar**d**v**a**rk

4

Dr. K. Fisher
Any problem solved!
1 Diving-in-the-Water
Birdsville 54321

Dear **Quietly Confident,**
I'm afraid this is an impossible challenge. You are used to burrowing in the sandy desert, but planet Earth is a rocky ball made up of three different layers. First, there is a rocky crust up to 40 miles (60 kilometers) thick. Next, there's a layer called the mantle, made of hot, melted rock almost 2,000 miles (3,000 kilometers) thick. Finally, in the center, there's a metal core, where it's too hot for any animal to survive. Tell your friends to suggest a different challenge. Why not show them how far you can burrow in a day?

Good luck!

Dr. K. Fisher

crust

mantle

core

Planet Earth

5

Here's an excited emu

Dear Dr. K. Fisher,

I'm an emu, and I live in Australia. My family here is small, but I've just heard some exciting news—I have lots of relatives that I've never met! They are called ostrich, and I'm told there is a strong family resemblance. I'm eager to get in touch. Any idea how I can trace them?

Looking for Family,
Down Under

THE OUTBACK
MAY 16
MAIL

Dr. K. Fisher

1 Diving-in-the-Water

Birdsville 54321

emu chicks

emu

6

Dr. K. Fisher
Any problem solved!
1 Diving-in-the-Water
Birdsville 54321

Dear **Looking for Family,**

It's true you are related to the ostrich, but you live on different continents. Continents are enormous pieces of land, and the world has seven of them altogether. They are divided from one another by Earth's oceans and seas. Ostrich live on the continent of Africa, while you live more than 5,000 miles (8,000 kilometers) away across the Indian Ocean, on the continent of Australia. I'm sorry that you won't be able to visit your relatives, but I hope you'll be pleased with the photo I'm sending. Now you can see the family resemblance for yourself!

All good wishes,

Dr. K. Fisher

ostrich

Turn the page for **more** about **Earth's continents and oceans . . .**

Dr. K. Fisher's Guide to Continents and Oceans

Earth's surface is covered with **seven** great land masses known as continents and **five huge** areas of water called oceans. Earth's surface can **be drawn** on a flat **map**, but Earth is really a round ball, which is better shown **with** a globe.

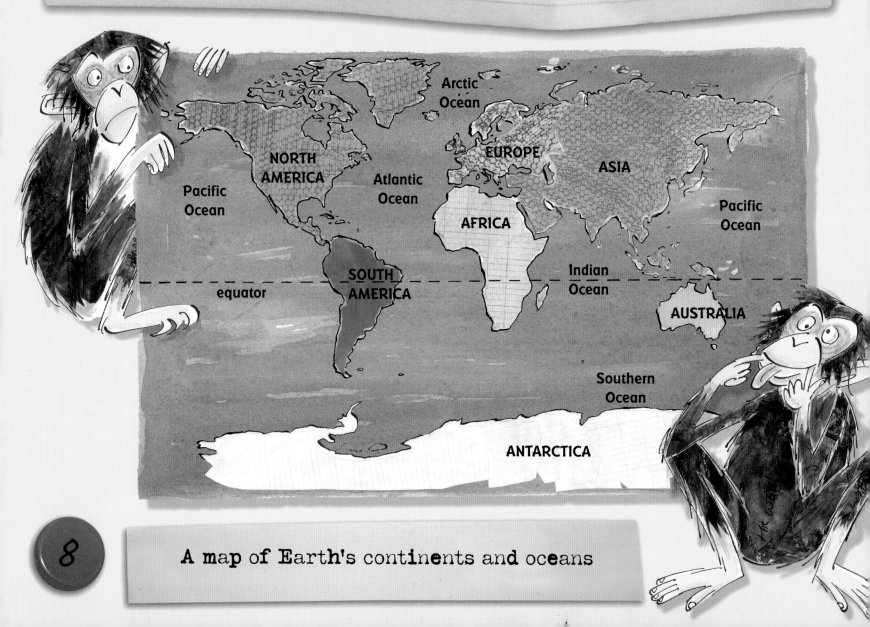

Arctic Ocean

NORTH AMERICA

EUROPE

ASIA

Pacific Ocean

Atlantic Ocean

AFRICA

Pacific Ocean

SOUTH AMERICA

Indian Ocean

equator

AUSTRALIA

Southern Ocean

ANTARCTICA

A map of Earth's continents and oceans

A globe is a round ball, just like Earth itself.

The two ends of Earth are called the North Pole and the South Pole.

On a globe, you can see only part of Earth at a time.

The equator is an imaginary line around the middle of Earth.

North Pole

ASIA

EUROPE

AFRICA

equator

to the South Pole

chimpanzee

Here's a snake that's feeling shaky

Warning Signs?

Dear Dr. K. Fisher,

I'm a viper, and I'm feeling uneasy. This week, as I've been moving through the forest, I've felt vibrations in the ground that seem to warn me of danger. The other animals haven't mentioned this, so maybe I'm imagining things. Please can you advise me?

Something's Wrong,
in the forest

viper

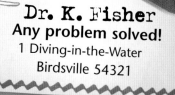

Dr. K. Fisher
Any problem solved!
1 Diving-in-the-Water
Birdsville 54321

monkeys

Dear **Something's Wrong,**

Snakes are sensitive creatures, so I suspect you are feeling small movements called tremors from deep underground. Our planet is not as solid as it seems. Its crust is broken up into slabs called plates, which float on the hot, melted rock below. In places where two plates meet, they can jolt one another. This causes earthquakes, which make the ground shake or even crack wide open. Some earthquakes are fairly gentle, but to be safe, find a strong tree and take shelter there.

Good luck!

Dr. K. Fisher

I'm fuming!

Dear Dr. K. Fisher,

I'm a chinchilla, and I live in the Andes mountains. This week I haven't slept a wink. Across the valley they're having a fireworks party—flames, sparks, and clouds of smoke are shooting into the sky. I enjoy fireworks as much as anyone, but four days and nights is overdoing it. What's happening to good manners these days?

Sleepless,
in South America

chinchillas

Dear **Sleepless,**

I suspect this isn't a fireworks party but an erupting volcano. A volcano is a special kind of mountain that sometimes explodes, sending hot melted rock, gases, and ash shooting into the air. The rock, called lava, comes from deep inside the Earth and spurts out through a hole, or vent, in the crust. In time, the volcano will quiet down, and the lava will cool to become solid rock. Active volcanoes erupt from time to time. This one is clearly at a safe distance, so you can stay in your burrow. If it were any closer, you might have to run from the poisonous gases and ash.

Yours,

Dr. K. Fisher

erupting volcano

lava — vent

volcano

hot magma underground

Turn the page for **more about mountains . . .**

13

Dr. K. Fisher's Guide to Mountains

Mountains are places where the ground rises steeply and is very high. Not all mountains are volcanoes, and many of them stretch over huge distances in long lines called ranges. They are wild places with spectacular scenery.

Valleys are more sheltered than the windy peaks.

bear

Melting snow and ice form mountain streams, which tumble through deep valleys.

In the summer, meadows are filled with flowers.

meadow

The highest peaks are always covered in snow. It is too cold for trees to grow there.

goose

The snow packs down to make icy glaciers, which move slowly down the slopes.

goat

Evergreen trees have sloping branches that shrug off the heavy snow.

Dr. K. Fisher's Top Tips

⭐ Mountains are rocky and bitterly cold. DON'T live here unless you are sure-footed and have a warm coat.

⭐ Birds, if you migrate long distances, DO use mountains as landmarks. Their snowy peaks are unmissable from the air.

⭐ Everyone, DO look and listen out for mountain streams. This is the cleanest water you'll ever drink.

15

which way to the ocean?

Dear Dr. K. Fisher,

I'm a young salmon, and I live in a mountain stream. My friend, a water vole, tells me that in a little while I will swim away on a journey to the ocean. It sounds exciting, but I need to know more. What will the journey be like? What happens if I lose my way? And what is the ocean?

Fishing for Answers,
in the stream

water vole

salmon

Dr. K. Fisher
Any problem solved!
1 Diving-in-the-Water
Birdsville 54321

Dear **Fishing for Answers,**

Baby salmon hatch in a river, but after a few years you swim downstream and spend part of your life in the ocean. The ocean is a huge area of water. Combined with seas, it covers two-thirds of Earth's surface. The ocean is a great place to live and grow because it is full of food. The journey is easy, and you won't get lost. Just follow your stream as it runs downhill. Soon it will join up with other streams and become a much larger river—and every river, however long, flows into the ocean eventually.

Bon voyage!

Dr. K. Fisher

Turn the page for
more about rivers . . .

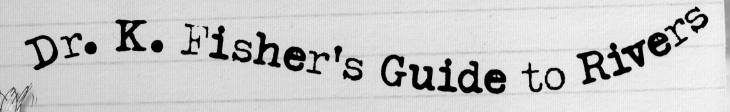

Dr. K. Fisher's Guide to Rivers

A river carries rainwater from the hills to the ocean. What starts out as a tiny trickle soon joins with other streams to make a fast-flowing river. As a river flows along, it changes the shape of the landscape.

hills

2. The trickle grows into a stream.

1. A spring bubbles out of the ground.

3. Streams join together to make a wider river.

Dr. K. Fisher's Top Tips

⭐ Rivers can carry big stones. Water animals,
DO watch out for these when you are swimming.

⭐ DON'T worry if a river is brown and muddy.
It just means it's carrying sand and soil.

⭐ After a heavy rain, rivers can flood. Land animals,
DO stay in reach of higher, drier ground.

4. The river flows slowly on flatter ground.

river

5. At the river's mouth, water flows into the ocean.

ocean

All dried up

Dear Dr. K. Fisher,

I'm a mussel, and I'm finding life hard. Twice a day, I'm covered by the ocean, which keeps me moist and supplies me with fresh food. But twice a day, the ocean disappears, and I'm left to dry out here on the rock with nothing between me and the gulls. Why does the water disappear, and how can I make it stay?

High and Dry,
beside the ocean

gull

clam

rocks at
low tide

mussel

20

Dr. K. Fisher
Any problem solved!
1 Diving-in-the-Water
Birdsville 54321

Dear **High and Dry,**

I'm afraid there's no way you can control the ocean. Twice a day, at high tide, it rises up the shore. Twice a day, at low tide, it sinks back down again. Tides are caused by the Moon, which has a force called gravity that pulls on our planet and its oceans. Tides make the shore a tricky place to live, but at least you live on the damp rocks. Hidden among them are rock pools, where ocean water collects at high tide, providing nonstop moisture and food. And don't be alarmed—your hard shell will protect you from the gulls.

With good wishes,

Dr. K. Fisher

crab

starfish

rocks at **high tide**

seaweed

21

Here's a chilly penguin

adult penguins

Cold in the colony

Dear Dr. K. Fisher,
I'm an emperor penguin chick, and I have a bad feeling about the place where I have hatched. It's a dark, icy wasteland with howling winds and snow. Although I have loving parents and live in a friendly colony, I feel like I'm at the end of the earth. Is there anything good about this place?

Shivering,
on the ice shelf

chicks huddling together

22

shrimp

Dr. K. Fisher
Any problem solved!
1 Diving-in-the-Water
Birdsville 54321

Dear **Shivering,**

You're quite right: you do live at the end of the earth, in an icy land around the South Pole. It's called Antarctica, and the climate there is very harsh. In the winter the temperature falls to -90° F (-70° C). But don't worry—you and the other penguins are well adapted to live in the cold. You have a layer of fat under your skin and thick feathers to keep you warm. You'll soon be swimming in the ocean, gobbling up juicy fish and shrimp. Then you won't want to swap your icy home for anywhere else on Earth.

Good luck!

Dr. K. Fisher

Turn the page for **more** about **the world's climates...**

Dr. K. Fisher's Guide to the World's Climates

Every part of the world has its own **weather pattern**, called its climate. In one place the climate may be **warm** and **wet**; in another, cold and dry. The climate affects the types of plants and animals that can **live there**.

desert

taiga (coniferous forest)

grassland

Very dry all year long and a difficult place for plants and animals to survive. Cacti and camels do well here.

Very cold winters and warm summers. The evergreen trees shelter reindeer and wolves.

Warm all year, with seasonal rains. Grasses provide food for antelope and wildebeests.

deciduous forest

polar land

rainforest

A mild climate with four seasons—spring, summer, fall, and winter. Trees lose their leaves in the winter.

Long, dark, freezing winters and short summers. Polar bears and seals live here.

Hot and wet all year long. The dense forests provide a home for monkeys, toucans, and jaguars.

Dr. K. Fisher's Top Tips

Summers too hot? Winters too cold? DO think about moving to the coast where the climate is milder and wetter than it is inland.

Feeling chilly? DO try moving to lower ground. The temperature is always cooler the higher up you are.

Over the years, climates can change. DO move to new areas if they become more suitable for you.

25

Bring back the light!

Dear Dr. K. Fisher,
I'm a cheetah cub, and I have a problem. Every afternoon, I go out hunting with my mother, brother, and sisters. I have a good time until the light fades, but then everything gets dark and spooky. I get worried in the dark—it frightens me. Where does the light go?

Don't Like the Dark,
on the grasslands

cheetah cub

Sun

Earth

nighttime

Dr. K. Fisher
Any problem solved!
1 Diving-in-the-Water
Birdsville 54321

Dear **Don't Like the Dark,**

Here on planet Earth, our lives follow a pattern of light days and dark nights. Our light comes from the Sun, a star that burns far away in space. Because Earth is a solid, spinning ball, light from the Sun reaches only one side of the planet at a time; the other side has night. As Earth spins around, the bright side moves out of the Sun and into the shadow of night. Nighttime is cool and quiet and nothing to be afraid of. Curl up and enjoy a good night's sleep—in the morning, the Sun will be back.

Best wishes,

Dr. K. Fisher

What on Earth?

space shuttle

Dear Dr. K. Fisher,

I'm a bald eagle living in Florida, and I've just seen something spectacular—a flying machine taking off from the ground and soaring into the sky! I hear it's exploring outer space. How cool is that? As someone who's migrated long distances, I feel sure I am suited to space exploration. Where should I start?

Space Pioneer,
in the pines

28

blue jays

Dr. K. Fisher
Any problem solved!
1 Diving-in-the-Water
Birdsville 54321

Dear **Space Pioneer,**

I am sorry to disappoint you, but you will never be able to explore space. Space is a harsh environment, and Earth may be the only place where animals and plants can survive. Our planet is just the right distance from the Sun, so it is neither too hot nor too cold. It has water, and it's protected by the atmosphere, a blanket of gases that contains the oxygen we need to survive. Millions of different creatures live on Earth. If you long to explore, why not spread your wings and fly around our wonderful home?

Happy travels!

Dr. K. Fisher

atmosphere

Earth

space

bald eagle

29

Glossary

atmosphere
The mixture of gases that surrounds Earth.

climate
The normal weather pattern in a particular part of the world.

coast
A stretch of land beside the ocean.

colony
A group of animals that live close together.

continent
One of the seven large land masses on Earth.

earthquake
A sudden movement of Earth's surface. It can cause a lot of damage.

environment
The natural surroundings in which animals, plants, and people live.

equator
An imaginary line around the middle of Earth.

gas
A very light, shapeless, often invisible substance. Air is a mixture of different gases.

globe
A map of the world in the shape of a ball, or the world itself.

gravity
An invisible force that pulls things toward the center of Earth. It is gravity that makes objects fall to the ground.

30

migrate
To move from one part of the world to another to spend part of the year there.

mountain
A high, rocky part of Earth's surface, much higher than a hill.

ocean
A very large area of salty water on the surface of Earth.

oxygen
A gas that is found in the air. All living things need oxygen to survive.

planet
A very large ball that moves around a star. Earth is a planet that moves around the Sun, our nearest star.

sea
A large area of salty water. Seas are smaller than oceans.

space
The area outside Earth's atmosphere where the stars and planets are.

spring
A place where water flows out of the ground.

stream
A small river.

temperature
A measurement of how hot or cold something is.

tide
The rise and fall of the ocean.

tremor
A small shake or wobble, or a slight earthquake.

vent
An opening in the ground.

vibrations
Shaking movements.

volcano
A mountain with a hole in the top, through which hot rock, lava, gases, steam, and dust are forced out from inside the Earth.

Index